RA Ieso

R.A. Ieso

saving

La guía del millonario
The millionaire's guide

introduction

In a world where financial success is often presented as an enigma reserved for the privileged few, the need arises for a practical and accessible guide that demonstrates that the path to wealth is within everyone's reach. "The Millionaire's Guide" is a detailed compendium of fundamental strategies and principles that will help you master the three cornerstones of economic growth: savings, investment and entrepreneurship.

In these pages, you will embark on a transformative journey that will take you from the basics of money management to advanced investing techniques and proven entrepreneurial strategies. Whether you're taking your first steps into the financial world or looking to take your wealth to the next level, this book is designed to be your trusted companion on the path to financial freedom and lasting success.

Through a combination of practical advice, inspiring examples, and practical exercises, you will learn how to cultivate solid financial habits, identify lucrative investment opportunities, and develop the mindset and skills necessary to become a successful entrepreneur. More than just a manual, "The Millionaire's Guide" is a comprehensive roadmap for those who aspire to reach the pinnacle of financial success and build a lasting legacy for generations to come.

Get ready to challenge your limiting beliefs, expand your financial horizons, and discover the unlimited potential that lies within you. With determination, discipline, and the right knowledge at your disposal, you are about to embark on a journey toward abundance and the realization of your most ambitious dreams. Welcome to "The Millionaire's Guide"!

Number one, Savings:

Point one. Strategies to save money on a daily basis.

In everyday life, we often face unexpected expenses and temptations to spend money on things we don't really need. However, with some simple strategies, we can learn to better manage our finances and save money in our daily lives. Below are some effective strategies to achieve this.

1. Establish a Budget:

- Create a monthly budget that includes all income and expenses.
- Prioritize essential expenses, such as food, housing, and transportation, and allocate specific amounts for each category.

•Limit discretionary spending, such as entertainment and unplanned purchases, establishing a monthly limit for these expenses.

2. Follow the 50-30-20 Rule:

- Allocate 50% of income to essential expenses, such as housing and utilities.
- Allocate 30% of income to discretionary expenses, such as entertainment and meals away from home.
- Reserve 20% of income for savings and long-term investment.

3. Buy with Intelligence:

- Compare prices before making large purchases and look for deals and discounts.
- Use coupons, discount apps and rewards programs to save in regular purchases.
- Avoid impulsive purchases and reflect before making a purchase to determine if it is really necessary.

4. Reduce Unnecessary Expenses:

- Delete subscriptions and memberships that are not used frequently.
- Renegotiate service contracts, such as internet and cell phone, to obtain lower rates.

•Reduce energy and water consumption at home through efficient use of appliances and the installation of water and energy saving devices.

5. Prepare Meals at Home:

- Plan weekly meals and make a shopping list to avoid eating out from home frequently.
- Cook in batches and freeze leftovers for ready-to-eat meals on the go. future.
- Use coupons and deals on groceries and buy generic products instead of expensive brands.

6. Save on Transportation:

- Use public transportation or carpooling instead of driving alone to reduce costs fuel and parking costs.
- Consider transportation alternatives, such as walking or bicycling, to short distances.
- Keep your car in good condition and drive efficiently to save fuel.

Conclusion: Implementing these strategies to save money on a daily basis can make a big difference in our personal finances in the long term. By being aware of our spending habits and making informed financial decisions, we can achieve our savings goals and have greater financial stability in the future.

Point two. Methods for establishing and maintaining an effective budget.

An effective budget is a fundamental tool to manage our personal finances successfully. It allows us to plan and control our income and expenses, helping us achieve our short and long-term financial objectives. Below are some practical methods for establishing and maintaining an effective budget.

1. Category-Based Budget Method:

- Identify all categories of expenses, such as housing, food, transportation, entertainment, debts, savings, etc.
- Assign an estimated amount to each category based on income and needs. financial priorities.
- Record actual expenses in each category and compare them to the budget assigned.
- Adjust the budget as necessary to maintain a balance between income and expenses.

2. 50-30-20 Method:

- Allocate 50% of income to essential expenses, such as housing, food and public services.

- Allocate 30% of income to discretionary expenses, such as entertainment, restaurants and non-essential shopping.

- Reserve 20% of income for long-term savings and investment, including paying debts and creating an emergency fund.

3. Zero Budget Method:

- Allocate each dollar of income to a specific category, so that it is not unallocated money.

- Prioritize needs over wants and adjust the budget to ensure that Income covers all planned expenses.

- Review and adjust the budget monthly to reflect changes in income and expenses.

4. Automatic Budget Method:

- Set up automatic payments for recurring expenses, like utility bills public funds, rent or mortgage, and contributions to savings and investment funds.

- Use financial management applications and tools that categorize automatically expenses and provide detailed reports on financial status.

- Set alerts or reminders to monitor the budget and avoid expenses excessive.

5. Objective-Based Budget Method:

- Set clear, measurable financial goals, such as saving for a savings fund. emergency, pay debts, buy a house, etc.

- Allocate specific financial resources for each objective and establish realistic deadlines to reach them.

- Closely monitor progress toward goals and adjust budget as necessary necessary to stay the course.

Conclusion: Whatever budgeting method you choose, the most important thing is to be consistent and disciplined in following it. Establishing an effective budget and maintaining it over time will provide you with greater financial clarity and help you make more informed decisions about your monetary resources, which in turn will bring you closer to your financial goals.

Point three. Useful tools and apps for tracking expenses and savings.

In the digital age, tracking expenses and savings has become more accessible thanks to a variety of tools and apps available on mobile devices and computers.

These tools not only simplify the process of keeping financial records, but also provide valuable insights to improve personal finance management.

1. Budget and Expense Tracking Apps:

- Mint: It is one of the most popular apps for budgeting and tracking money. bills. Allows you to sync bank accounts, credit cards, and investments to automatically track expenses, categorize transactions, and set custom budgets.

- YNAB (You Need a Budget): YNAB focuses on allocating every dollar to a purpose specific, helping users prioritize expenses, reduce debt and achieve their long-term financial goals.

- PocketGuard: Provides an overview of daily finances, with a focus on money available after taking into account recurring expenses and savings. It also provides alerts on outstanding invoices and tips to optimize finances.

2. Automatic Savings Applications:

- Acorns: This app rounds purchases to the next dollar and automatically invests the change into diversified investment portfolios, helping users save and invest passively.

- Digit: Digit analyzes users' spending patterns and automatically transfers small amounts of money to a separate savings account, using a smart algorithm to minimize the impact on the daily budget.

- Qapital: Allows users to set custom rules to save automatically, such as saving a percentage of each paycheck or saving every time they make a purchase.

3. Financial Analysis Applications:

- Personal Capital: Provides a comprehensive view of finances, including tracking investment, retirement planning and portfolio analysis, allowing users to make more informed financial decisions.

- Money Dashboard: Allows users to view all their bank accounts and credit cards. credit in one place, and offers detailed analysis of spending and financial trends to help identify areas for improvement.

- Tiller Money: Automate Google Sheets or Excel spreadsheets so that users Users can customize their own financial reports and keep track of their finances in more detail.

Conclusion: Using tools and apps to track expenses and savings can greatly simplify personal financial management. From setting budgets to automating savings and investments, these tools offer a variety of features to suit individual needs and preferences. By leveraging these tools effectively, users can take control of their finances and work toward greater financial stability and security in the future.

Point four. Tips to avoid unnecessary expenses and control impulsive purchases.

Unnecessary spending and impulsive purchases can negatively affect our personal finances, causing us to spend more than we earn and making it difficult to achieve our financial goals. However, with some practical strategies and tips, we can learn to control these habits and make more conscious financial decisions.

1. Set a Budget:

- Define a detailed monthly budget that includes your expected income and expenses.
- Allocate specific amounts for each spending category, such as food, transportation, entertainment, etc.
- Check your budget regularly and adjust your spending as necessary to keep you within your limits.

2. Make a Shopping List:

- Before you go shopping, make a detailed list of the items you need to buy.
- Stay true to your list and avoid purchasing items that are not on it, unless are really necessary.
- Consider setting a time limit for your purchases to avoid wandering around shops and fall into unnecessary temptations.

3. Plan your Purchases in Advance:

- Avoid impulse purchases by planning in advance what you need to buy.
- Wait 24 hours before making a major purchase to allow time to consider if you really need or want the item.
- Do your research and compare prices at different stores or online to get the best possible offer.

4. Use the Waiting List Method:

- Create a wish list for items you don't need immediately but would you like to buy in the future.
- Wait a certain period of time before purchasing an item on your wish list. wishes to make sure you really need it and it's not just a momentary impulse.
- Regularly reevaluate your wish list and remove items that no longer interest you. or need.

5. Practice the 30 Day Rule:

- Before buying something you don't need right away, wait at least 30 days.

- During this time, reflect on whether you really need or want the item and whether you can justify its cost.

- If after 30 days you still want the item and can pay for it within your budget, consider purchasing it.

6. Keep a Record of Expenses:

- Keep detailed records of all your expenses, including small purchases and impulse purchases.

- Regularly review your spending record to identify spending patterns and areas in which you can reduce unnecessary expenses.

- Use expense tracking apps to simplify this process and get Detailed reports on your spending habits.

7. Reflect on your Purchase Motivations:

- Before making an impulse purchase, reflect on your motivations behind the purchase. buys.

- Ask yourself if you really need the item or if you are trying to fill a void. emotional or satisfy a momentary impulse.

- Look for healthy alternatives to satisfy your emotional needs, such as doing exercise, practice meditation, or talk to a friend.

Conclusion: Controlling unnecessary spending and avoiding impulsive purchases requires discipline and self-control, but with practice and perseverance, it is possible to develop healthier financial habits. By setting a budget, making shopping lists, planning purchases in advance, and reflecting on our purchasing motivations, we can make more conscious financial decisions and work toward greater long-term financial stability.

Number 2. Investment:

What is an investment?

Investment is the act of dedicating financial resources, time or effort to an activity with the expectation of obtaining a future benefit. In the financial context, investment involves placing money in financial assets, such as stocks, bonds, real estate, mutual funds, among others, with the aim of generating income or increasing the value of the invested capital.

The investment can be made with different objectives, such as:

1. **Generate income**: Some investments, such as bonds that pay periodic interest or stocks that pay dividends, can provide a steady stream of income.

2. **Capital appreciation:** Many investments have the potential to increase in value over time, allowing investors to make profits by selling those assets at a price higher than the initial cost.

3. **Diversification:** Investing in a variety of assets can help spread the risk and protect against significant losses in the event that an investment is not successful.

4. **Achieve long-term financial goals:** Long-term investments, such as Investing in retirement funds or investing in college education can help people achieve specific financial goals in the future.

It is important to keep in mind that investing carries risks, and not all investments guarantee profits. Investors should conduct extensive research, diversify their portfolios, and consider their risk tolerance before making investments. Additionally, it is essential to have a solid financial plan and consult with qualified financial advisors if necessary.

First point. Introduction to investment basics (stocks, bonds, mutual funds, etc.).

Investing is a fundamental part of personal financial management, and understanding the basics of different types of investments is crucial to making informed financial decisions and building a diversified portfolio. Below, we'll explore some of the basics of investing, including stocks, bonds, mutual funds, and more.

1. Actions:

- Shares represent partial ownership of a company.

- By purchasing shares, investors acquire a stake in the property and therefore Therefore, they are entitled to a portion of the company's profits and decisions.

- The value of the shares may fluctuate based on the financial performance of the company, market conditions and other factors.

2. Bonuses:

- Bonds are debt instruments issued by governments, companies or other entities to raise funds.

- By purchasing a bond, the investor is lending money to the issuer in exchange for regular interest and repayment of principal at maturity.

- Bonds can offer fixed or variable interest payments and have different terms expiration.

3. Mutual Funds:

- Mutual funds are investment vehicles that pool money from multiple investors to buy a diversified portfolio of stocks, bonds or other assets.

- Mutual funds are managed by professional fund managers, who They make investment decisions on behalf of investors.

- Mutual fund investors own shares of the fund and share in the profits and losses proportional to your investment.

4. ETFs (Exchange-Traded Funds):

- ETFs are publicly traded investment funds that trade like stocks.

- Like mutual funds, ETFs invest in a diversified portfolio of assets, but can be bought and sold at any time during market trading hours.

- ETFs typically have lower costs than traditional mutual funds and offer greater liquidity and flexibility.

5. Real Estate:

- Investing in real estate involves purchasing properties, such as houses, apartments, commercial premises or land, with the objective of generating rental income or value appreciation.

- Real estate investors can earn regular income through rents and make a profit by selling the property at a higher price than the initial cost.

Conclusion: Understanding the basics of investing is essential to building a solid investment portfolio and achieving long-term financial goals. By knowing the different types of assets available, their characteristics and associated risks, investors can make informed decisions and diversify their portfolio to maximize return potential and minimize risk. It is important to conduct thorough research, consult with financial advisors, and stay up-to-date on market trends to make prudent and successful investment decisions.

Point two. Long-term investment strategies.

Long-term investment strategies are planned and disciplined approaches to building and growing an investment portfolio over time. These strategies are designed to maximize returns and minimize risk as the investor works toward long-term financial goals, such as retirement, a child's college education, or purchasing a home. Here are some common long-term investing strategies:

1. **Portfolio Diversification:**

   - Diversification is a fundamental strategy to reduce the risk of a portfolio.

   - It consists of distributing assets between different asset classes (stocks, bonds, real estate, etc.) and industrial sectors to avoid putting all eggs in one basket.

   - Diversification helps mitigate the negative impact of market volatility on a given asset class and can improve long-term risk-adjusted returns.

2. Regular and long-term investment:

   - Regular and consistent investing over time, known as investing Systematically, it is a powerful strategy to harness the power of compound interest.

   - Investors can establish a periodic investment plan, such as contributions monthly to an investment fund or retirement account, regardless of market fluctuations.

   - This strategy helps smooth out market fluctuations and reduce the risk of Timing the market by averaging the purchase cost of assets over time.

3. **Buy and Hold:**

   - The buy and hold strategy involves purchasing stocks or other assets and hold them for an extended period, regardless of short-term market fluctuations.

   - This strategy is based on the belief that, in the long term, the market tends to grow and provide solid returns, so investors can benefit from holding their investments for the long term.

   - Buy and hold is a passive strategy that requires patience and discipline to Resist the temptation to sell in response to market volatility.

4. Periodic portfolio rebalancing:

- Portfolio rebalancing involves adjusting your asset allocation periodically to maintain diversification and risk objectives.

- As assets fluctuate in value, the portfolio's asset allocation can deviate from the original goals, so it is important to rebalance regularly to restore the desired allocation.
- This strategy allows investors to buy undervalued assets and sell overvalued assets, which can increase long-term returns and reduce risk.

5. Investment in high-quality long-term assets:

- Focus on investing in high-quality assets, such as solid companies with solid financial fundamentals, investment grade bonds and quality real estate.
- Investing in high-quality assets can provide a steady flow of long-term income and growth, minimizing the risk of significant losses.

In short, long-term investment strategies are designed to help investors build wealth sustainably over time by harnessing the power of compound interest, diversifying the portfolio, and maintaining a disciplined and patient approach. It is important to keep in mind that all investments carry some degree of risk and that each investor should tailor their strategy to their specific financial objectives, risk tolerance and time horizon.

Point three. Tips for beginners on how to start investing.

Getting started with investing may seem overwhelming to beginners, but with the right guidance and a gradual approach, it can be a rewarding and beneficial experience. Here are some tips for beginners on how to start investing:

1. Set your financial goals:

- Before starting to invest, identify your short, medium and long financial goals. term. Are you investing for retirement, to buy a house or to finance your children's education? Setting clear goals will help you determine your investment horizon and risk tolerance.

2. Learn the basics of investing:

- Familiarize yourself with the different types of investment assets, such as stocks, bonds, mutual funds, ETFs, real estate, etc. Understanding the basics will help you make informed decisions about where and how to invest your money.

3. Financial education:

- Invest time in educating yourself on the principles of investing and personal finance. read books, follow financial blogs, listen to podcasts, and attend investment seminars or webinars. The more you learn, the more confident you will be in your investment decisions.

4. Set a budget and save regularly:

- Before investing, make sure you have a solid budget and emergency fund established. Regularly save a portion of your income to invest, and make sure you have enough liquidity to cover unforeseen expenses before committing to long-term investments.

5. Start with simple investments:

- For beginners, it is advisable to start with simple, low-cost investments. risk, such as index funds or ETFs that track the performance of the broader market. These options are easy to understand and offer instant diversification.

6. Use appropriate investment accounts:

- Open a brokerage account or online investment account that suits your needs and objectives. You can choose between traditional brokerage accounts, retirement accounts like IRAs or 401(k), or online investment accounts with robo-advisors.

7. Diversify your portfolio:

- Don't put all your eggs in one basket. Diversify your portfolio by investing in different asset types and sectors to reduce risk and maximize long-term returns.

8. Maintain patience and discipline:

- Investing is a long-term journey and it is normal to experience ups and downs in the market. Stay calm during fluctuations and avoid making impulsive decisions based on fear or emotion. Maintain a long-term perspective and maintain discipline in your investment strategy.

9. Consult a financial advisor if necessary:

- If you're feeling overwhelmed or unsure about your investment decisions, consider looking into Professional guidance from a certified financial advisor. An advisor can help you create a personalized investment plan and provide expert guidance based on your individual circumstances.

In short, getting started investing can be challenging, but with the right education, careful planning, and patience, you can build a solid investment portfolio that helps you achieve your long-term financial goals. Remember that the key to success in investing is consistency, discipline and making informed decisions.

Point four. How to diversify an investment portfolio.

Diversifying an investment portfolio is a fundamental strategy to reduce risk and maximize long-term returns. Diversification involves spreading funds across different asset types and investment classes to avoid excessive concentration in a single investment and mitigate the negative impact of adverse market events. Here's a guide on how to diversify an investment portfolio:

1. Allocate assets into different investment classes:

- Spread your funds across different asset classes, such as stocks, bonds, assets roots, raw materials and cash. Each asset class has different risk and return characteristics, allowing for effective diversification.

2. Diversify within each asset class:

- Within each asset class, such as stocks or bonds, diversify further by choosing a variety of investments. For example, in stocks, you can invest in different industry sectors or geographic regions to reduce market-specific risk.

3. Use different investment styles:

- Consider diversifying through different investment styles, such as emerging market growth, value, revenue and opportunities. Each investment style has different characteristics and can perform better in different market conditions.

4. Invest in different sizes of companies:

- Diversify your portfolio by investing in companies of different sizes, from large capitalization companies to small and medium-sized companies. Companies of different sizes may have different risk and return profiles, which can help balance your portfolio.

5. Consider international investments:

- Invest a portion of your portfolio in international markets to gain exposure to different economies and currencies. International diversification can help reduce the risk associated with excessive exposure to a single market or country.

6. Invest in uncorrelated assets:

- Look for assets that have a low correlation with each other, meaning they are not move in the same direction in response to market events. Investing in uncorrelated assets can help reduce overall portfolio risk and smooth out market fluctuations.

7. Periodically rebalance your portfolio:

- Regularly review your portfolio and adjust asset allocation as necessary to maintain your diversification goals. Periodic rebalancing helps ensure your portfolio remains aligned with your risk tolerance and long-term financial goals.

8. Consider alternative investments:

- Explore alternative investments, such as hedge funds, private real estate, private equity or commodities, to further diversify your portfolio and add additional sources of potential return and protection against traditional market volatility.

In short, diversifying an investment portfolio is essential to reduce risk and maximize long-term returns. By spreading funds across different asset classes, investment styles, company sizes and geographic regions, you can build a balanced and resilient portfolio that adapts to a variety of market conditions and helps you achieve your financial goals.TT

Number 3-Entrepreneurship:

What is entrepreneurship?

Entrepreneurship refers to the process of starting, developing and managing a business with the goal of creating value, whether in the form of products, services, employment or economic benefits. Entrepreneurship involves taking risks, seeking opportunities, and using resources innovatively to solve problems, meet market needs, or take advantage of new trends.

Entrepreneurs are individuals who lead this process, identifying business opportunities, developing creative ideas, organizing resources and taking responsibility for making their vision become a reality. Entrepreneurship can manifest itself in a wide range of forms, from launching a new technology startup to creating a small local business, and even within existing organizations through intrapreneurship initiatives.

Entrepreneurship is a key driver for innovation, economic growth and job creation in many societies. By fostering creativity, resilience and the ability to adapt, entrepreneurship plays a crucial role in transforming industries, generating wealth and improving people's quality of life. Additionally, entrepreneurship can foster competition, diversity, and collaboration in the marketplace, benefiting consumers and society at large.

Point one. Steps to start your own business.

Starting your own business is an exciting and challenging step that can bring your business dreams to reality. Here I present a basic guide of the steps you can follow to start your own business:

1. **Reflect and define your business idea:**
   - Identify your skills, passions and interests.
   - Research the market to find opportunities and unmet needs.
   - Clearly define what products or services you will offer and what differentiates them from the competence.

2. **Make a business plan:**
   - Develop a detailed plan that includes your business concept, market analysis, marketing strategies, organizational structure, financial projections and initial budget.

- This plan will be your guide for the development and growth of your company, as well as a tool to obtain financing if necessary.

3   Investigate financial viability:

- Evaluate how much capital you need to start and maintain your business until it is profitable.
- Consider how you will finance your business: personal savings, loans, investors, crowdfunding, etc.
- Calculate your startup costs and operating expenses, as well as your potential sources of income.

4   Register your business:

- Choose an appropriate legal structure for your business (e.g. sole proprietorship, society, corporation).
- Register your company name and obtain the necessary permits and licenses to operate legally in your location.

5   Develop a brand identity:

- Create a business name and logo that represent your business and differentiate it in the market.
- Design an online presence with a professional website and social media profiles relevant to your industry.

6   Set up your operations:

- Establish a suitable workspace and acquire the equipment and tools necessary to operate your business.
- Define your internal processes, policies and procedures to ensure efficiency and consistency in the delivery of your products or services.

7   Hire and train staff (if necessary):

- Identify the key functions and responsibilities you need to cover in your company.
- Hire people with the right skills and experience to help you achieve your business goals.
- Provide ongoing training and development for your team to keep them motivated and productive.

8   Promote your business:

- Implement marketing strategies to publicize your company and attract customers potentials.
- Use a combination of digital and traditional marketing tactics, such as networking social media, online advertising, direct mail, networking events, etc.

9.   Measure and adjust:

- Establish key performance metrics to evaluate the success of your business.
- Regularly monitor your income, expenses, sales and other relevant metrics to identify areas of improvement.
- Make adjustments to your business plan as necessary to adapt to the changing market conditions and achieve your long-term goals.

10. Persist and adapt:

- The path to business success can be full of challenges and obstacles. Maintain a positive mindset and persevere through setbacks.
- Be willing to adapt and pivot when necessary to stay relevant and the competitiveness of your business in a constantly changing business environment.

By following these steps and maintaining focus and determination, you will be on the right path to successfully starting and growing your own business. Remember that every business is unique, so adapt these steps to your specific circumstances and don't be afraid to seek help when you need it!

Point two. Tips for developing an effective business plan.

Developing an effective business plan is essential to establishing a solid foundation and guiding the growth of your company. Here are some key tips for creating a business plan that is comprehensive, realistic and useful:

1. **Investigate thoroughly:**
- Before you start writing, do extensive research on the market, industry and competition. Understanding the environment in which your business will operate will help you make more informed decisions and identify opportunities and challenges.

2. Keep the focus on your audience:

- Keep in mind who your business plan is aimed at. If you are looking financing, your plan should be more detailed and focused on financial projections. If it is for internal use, you can focus more on operational and tactical strategies.

3. **Be clear and concise:**
- Avoid unnecessary technical jargon and use clear, easy-to-understand language. keep your business plan concise and focused on the most important aspects of your company.

4. Includes key sections:

- Make sure you cover the fundamental elements in your business plan, such as description of your company, market analysis, marketing strategy, organizational structure, financial plan and projections, among others.

5. Be realistic in your financial projections:

- Financial projections are a crucial part of your business plan. make sure base them on solid data and make realistic assumptions. Don't exaggerate your income or minimize your expenses; This could affect the credibility of your plan.

6 Identify and address risks:

Recognize the possible risks and challenges your company could face, and describe how you plan to mitigate them. This shows investors and lenders that you have considered the obstacles and have a plan to overcome them.

7 Showcase your unique value proposition:

- Highlight what makes your company unique and how you plan to differentiate yourself from the rest. competence. This can include your product or service, your marketing approach, your team, your technology, etc.

8 Be flexible:

A business plan is not a static sheet; must be flexible and customizable Market circumstances change and your company evolves. Regularly review and update your plan to reflect changes and new opportunities.

9 Get feedback and review:

- Before finalizing your business plan, get feedback from people you trust, mentors, business advisors or other industry experts. Their insights can help you identify areas for improvement and make your plan more robust.

10. Make a powerful executive summary:

- The executive summary is the first section that readers will read of your plan. business, so make sure it is compelling and attractive. Summarize the key aspects of your company, your objectives, your strategy and why your business will be successful.

By following these tips and taking the time and effort to develop a well-thought-out and comprehensive business plan, you will be better prepared to meet the challenges and take advantage of the opportunities that arise on the path to business success.

Point three. How to manage the challenges and risks associated with entrepreneurship.

Managing the challenges and risks associated with entrepreneurship is an integral part of the entrepreneurial journey. Here are some strategies to face and overcome these challenges:

1 Maintain a positive mindset:

- Accepting from the beginning that there will be challenges and risks will help you face them with a positive attitude. View obstacles as opportunities to learn and grow, rather than insurmountable obstacles.

2. Plan and anticipate challenges:

- Conduct a thorough analysis of the possible challenges and risks you could face in your business. Identify how they could affect your operations and develop contingency plans to handle them if they arise.

3 Set clear and realistic goals:

- Define clear and achievable goals for your business. This will help you keep the focus and motivation, even when faced with challenges. Break your goals into smaller, achievable milestones to keep you on track for success.

4 Create a support network:

- Seek support from others in the business community, whether through networking groups, mentors, coaches, or friends and family to provide encouragement and emotional support during difficult times.

5 Develop problem-solving skills:

- Learn to approach problems proactively and creatively. Focus on find solutions instead of focusing on the problems themselves. Sometimes challenges can become opportunities to innovate and improve your business.

6 Manage your finances wisely:

- Keep tight control over your finances and make sure you have enough capital to cover operating expenses and face unforeseen events. Set a realistic budget and regularly review your financial statements to identify possible areas for improvement.

7 Cultivate resilience:

- Resilience is the ability to recover quickly from setbacks and adapt to changing situations. Cultivate this skill by practicing self-compassion, maintaining a flexible mindset, and learning from your past experiences.

8 Seek constant learning:

- Never stop learning and improving. Stay up to date with market trends, Attend seminars, conferences and workshops relevant to your industry, and look for opportunities to expand your skills and knowledge.

9 Learn to delegate:

- Recognize that you can't do everything yourself and learn to delegate tasks to others. Build a strong team and trust them to help you face challenges and overcome obstacles along the way.

10. Maintain a balance between work and personal life:

- It is important to take care of your physical and emotional well-being while managing your business. Spend time doing activities that help you relax and recharge, such as exercise, meditation, spending time with friends and family, and enjoying your hobbies.

By implementing these strategies and adopting a proactive and resilient mindset, you will be better prepared to face the challenges and risks associated with entrepreneurship and achieve success in your business.

Point four. Resources and tools for entrepreneurs.

Entrepreneurs have access to a wide range of resources and tools that can help them develop, launch and grow their businesses. Here is a list of useful resources and tools for entrepreneurs:

1. **Startup incubators and accelerators:** These organizations offer programs support, mentoring, co-working space and connections with investors to help entrepreneurs drive the growth of their startups.

2. **Crowdfunding platforms**: Websites like Kickstarter, Indiegogo and GoFundMe They allow entrepreneurs to raise funds for their projects through donations or investments from people interested in supporting their ideas.

3. **Coworking spaces:** Shared workspaces provide a collaborative environment where entrepreneurs can work, connect with other professionals and access resources such as meeting rooms and networking events.

4. **Mentoring programs**: Mentoring programs match entrepreneurs with experienced professionals who can offer personalized guidance, advice and support to help them overcome challenges and make informed decisions.

5. **Online learning platforms:** Websites like Coursera, Udemy, and LinkedIn Learning offer online courses on a wide variety of business topics, from digital marketing and project management to finance and product development.

6. **Business management tools:** Business management software and applications such as Trello, Asana, Slack, and Google Workspace help entrepreneurs organize projects, communicate with teams and collaborators, and manage tasks and documents efficiently.

7. **Accounting and finance software**: Tools like QuickBooks, FreshBooks and Wave allows entrepreneurs to track income and expenses, generate invoices, manage taxes and maintain a clear view of the financial health of their business.

8. **E-commerce platforms**: For entrepreneurs who want to sell online products, platforms such as Shopify, WooCommerce and BigCommerce offer solutions to create and manage virtual stores easily and efficiently.

9. **Social networks and digital marketing tools:** Platforms like Facebook, Instagram, Twitter, LinkedIn, and YouTube are powerful tools for promoting products and services, engaging with potential customers, and building a strong brand online.

10. **Online Forums and Communities:** Websites and social media groups like Reddit, Quora, and LinkedIn Groups provide spaces where entrepreneurs can ask questions, share experiences, and learn from each other.

11. Business Events and Conferences: Attending entrepreneurship-related events and conferences offers opportunities to network, learn from industry experts, and gain inspiration to propel your business forward.

These are just a few examples of the many resources and tools available to entrepreneurs. By taking advantage of these opportunities and actively seeking support and guidance, entrepreneurs can increase their chances of success in the business world.

Gratitude

Before we dive into the pages of this book, I want to take a moment to express my sincere thanks to you, dear reader.

Thank you for embarking on this journey toward financial knowledge and personal growth. Your dedication and commitment to your own development are the driving force behind every word written in these pages.

I sincerely appreciate your trust in choosing this book as your guide in your quest for financial freedom and success. I hope you find in it the inspiration, knowledge and practical tools you need to achieve your goals and aspirations.

Your willingness to explore new ideas and pursue your dreams is a constant reminder of the transformative power that resides within each of us. May this book give you the clarity, motivation, and direction you need to chart your own path to abundance and personal fulfillment.

Once again, thank you for your trust and dedication. May this journey be the first of many steps towards a bright and prosperous future!

With gratitude,

[RA leso]

www.ingramcontent.com/pod-product-compliance
Lightning Source LLC
Chambersburg PA
CBHW081022240526
45471CB00018B/3951